PIANO / VOCAL / GUITAR

THE GABE DIXON BAND

T0078961

http://www.gabedixonband.com
http://www.myspace.com/gabedixonband
Management: Direct Management Group, Inc.
Dana Collins & Steve Jensen & Martin Kirkup

ISBN 978-1-4234-6888-2

HAL•LEONARD®
CORPORATION

7777 W. BLUEMOUND RD. P.O. BOX 13819 MILWAUKEE, WI 53213

In Australia Contact:
Hal Leonard Australia Pty. Ltd.
4 Lentara Court
Cheltenham, Victoria, 3192 Australia
Email: ausadmin@halleonard.com.au

Visit Hal Leonard Online at
www.halleonard.com

DISAPPEAR

Words and Music by GABE DIXON
and TY STEVENS

dis - ap - pear. _____

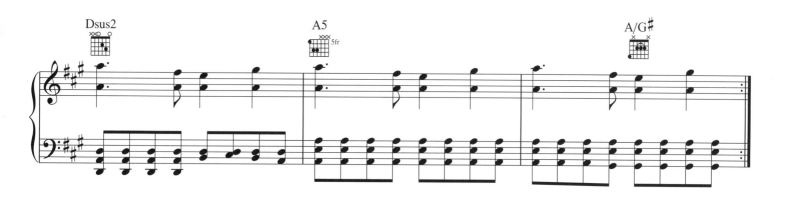

Can we __ dis - __ ap - pear? __

Can we __ dis -

- ap - pear? __

Can we di—, ____

FIVE MORE HOURS

Words and Music by GABE DIXON
and DAN WILSON

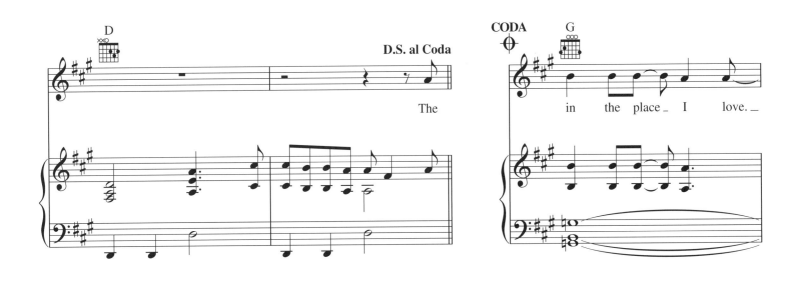

D.S. al Coda

CODA

The

in the place _ I love. _

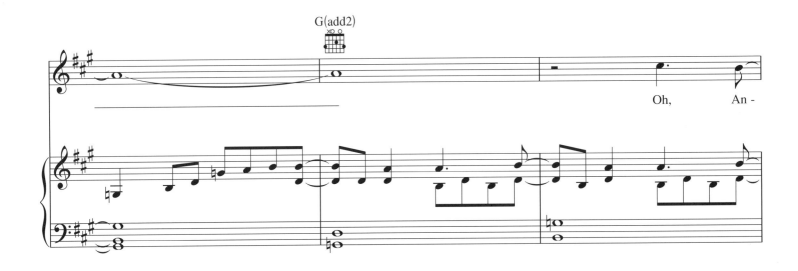

Oh, An -

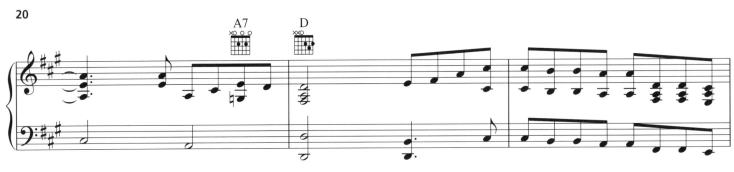

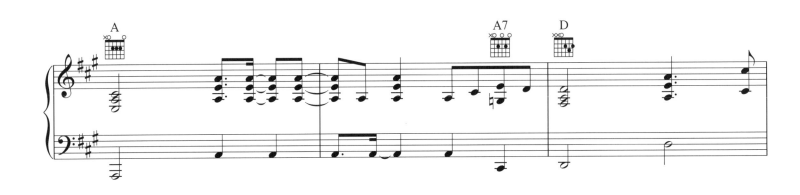

An - gel stay __ with me, _____ yeah, _ yeah. _

FURTHER THE SKY

Words and Music by GABE DIXON
and TIA SILLERS

When you don't __ know __ where you're go-
wish I __ could give __ you __ the an-

-ing __ and you don't know __ why,
-swers __ in pa-per and __ ink.

it feels like an-oth-er day is bleed-
I wish I could stop __ all __ the tears __

fur - ther the sky; ___ the more miles you walk, ___ the

long - er the road; ___ the steep - er you climb, ___ the

hard - er you stand ___ to ___ fall; ___ the

strong - er you get, ___ the heav - i - er the load. ___

The high-er, oh, the high-er, oh, the high-

-er that you reach, ___ the fur-ther, oh, the fur-ther, oh, the fur-

The big - ger the dream, ___ the rough - er the ride; ___

___ the tru - er the love, ___ the deep - er the ache; ___

_____ the blind - er the faith, ___ the tough - er the go. ___

the strong - er you get, ___ the heav-i-er the load. __

ALL WILL BE WELL

Words and Music by GABE DIXON
and DAN WILSON

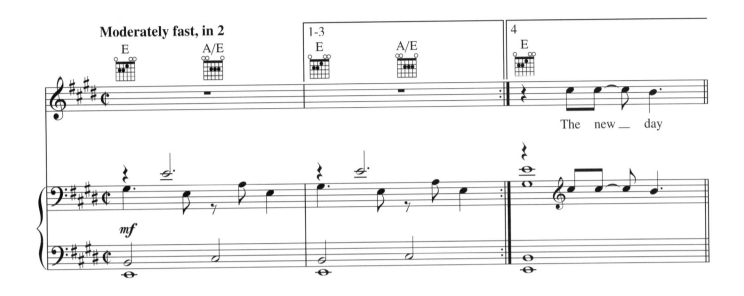

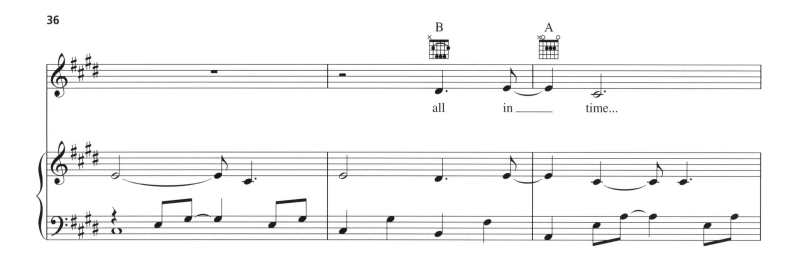

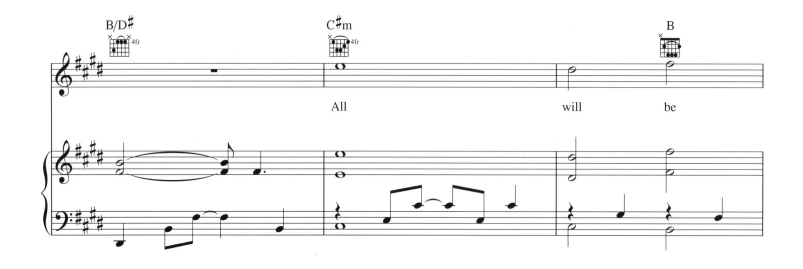

You can ask____ me how,____ but

on - ly time___ will tell.____

FIND MY WAY

Words and Music by GABE DIXON
and DAN WILSON

I don't mean to trou-ble your mind; ___ I'm just try-ing to find ___ my way

All those plans that I made for my-self, ___ I've got no-bod-y else ___ to lean

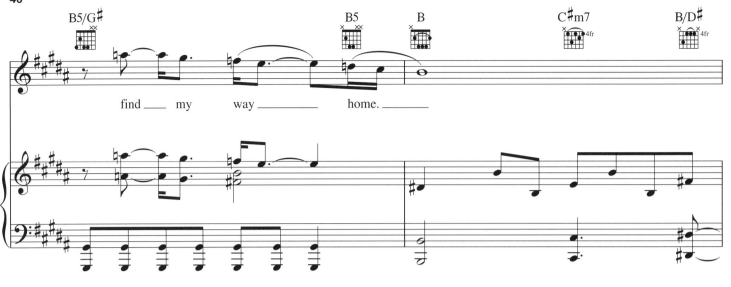

find ___ my ___ way _____ home. _____

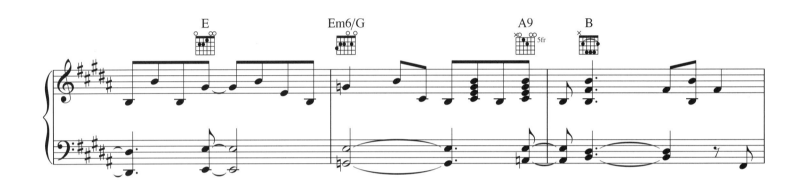

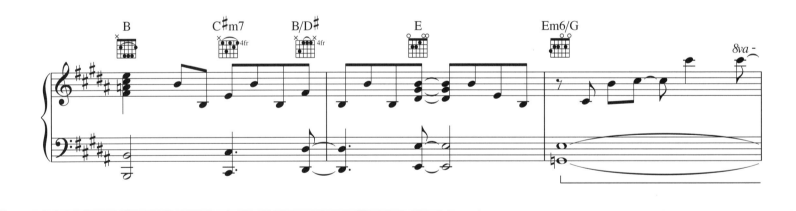

Slower, forcefully

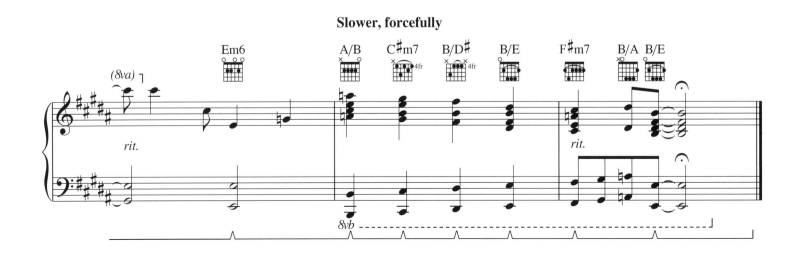

TILL YOU'RE GONE

Words and Music by GABE DIXON
and DYLAN ALTMAN

lis - ten, ba - by, when I say, "Let's

keep on keep - in' on till you're gone."

I'll be right here.

FAR FROM HOME

Words and Music by GABE DIXON
and JON McLAUGHLIN

EVER AFTER YOU

Words and Music by GABE DIXON
and WAYNE KIRKPATRICK

Eas - y come and eas - y go has nev - er been the case.
There is no psy-chol - o - gy, and no a - mount of prayers

Dreams of you are hard to e - rase.
that can cure the pain when you're not there.

AND THE WORLD TURNED

Words and Music by GABE DIXON
and TIA SILLERS

Moderately fast, expressively

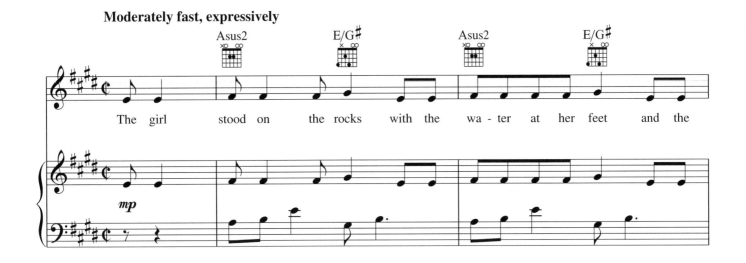

The girl stood on the rocks with the wa-ter at her feet and the

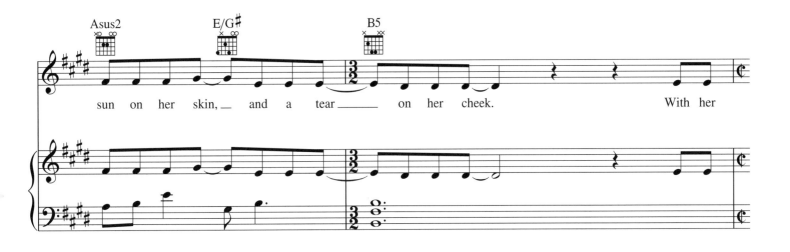

sun on her skin, __ and a tear _____ on her cheek. With her

hand at her chest and the wind in her hair, __ un-der-neath her breath, like a

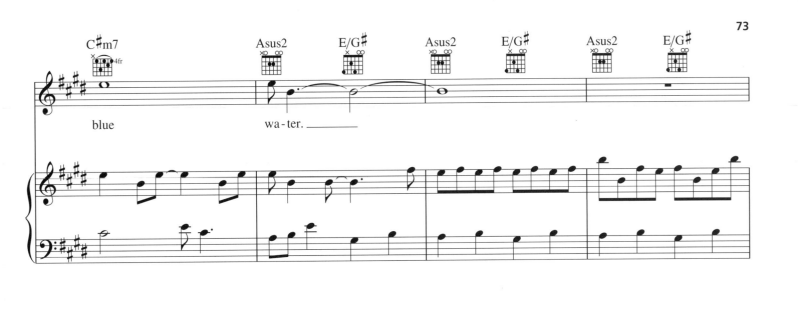

blue   wa-ter. _____

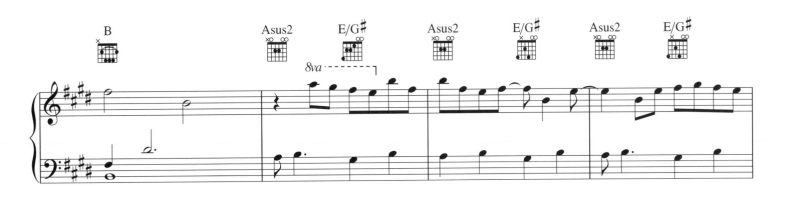

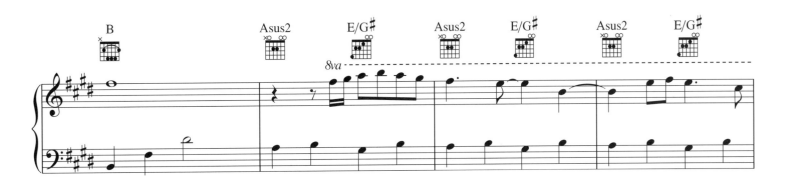

SIRENS

Words and Music by
GABE DIXON

Moderately fast

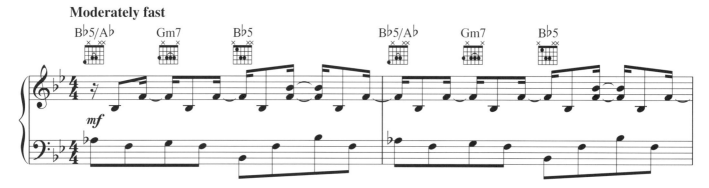

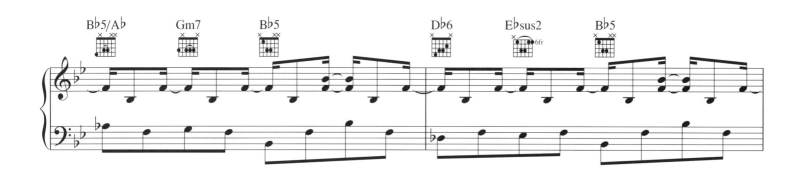

Moderately

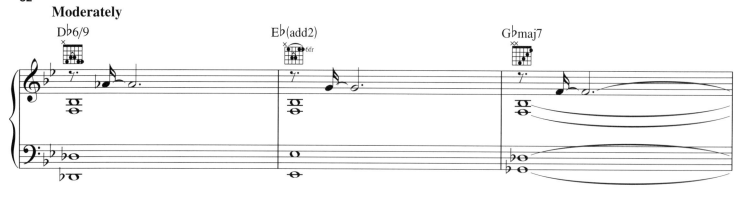

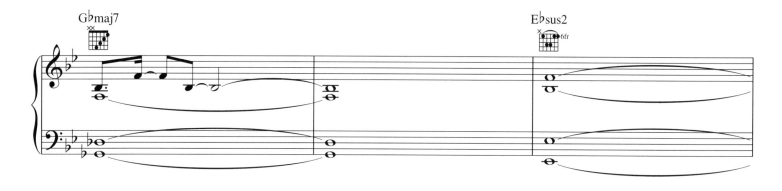

Tempo I

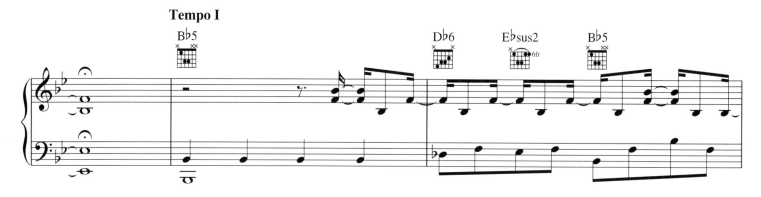

BABY DOLL

Words and Music by GABE DIXON
and BEN FUNDIS

take your cof - fee dif - f'rent - ly ___ each day.

You

Recorded a half step higher.